How to D Cat and Dog

Written and illustrated by Shoo Rayner

Contents

Collins

How to draw Cat

Start with a big,
round shape for
the head.

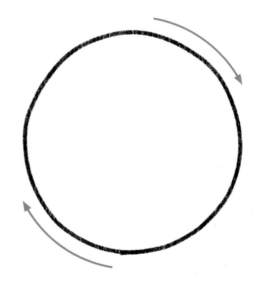

Draw a line up and down on the left side to make a triangle shape.

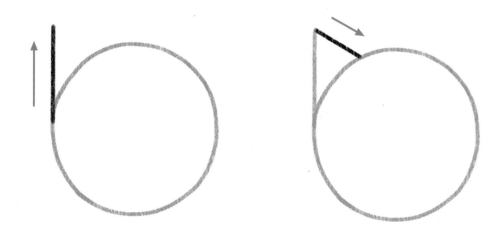

Draw another triangle on the right side.

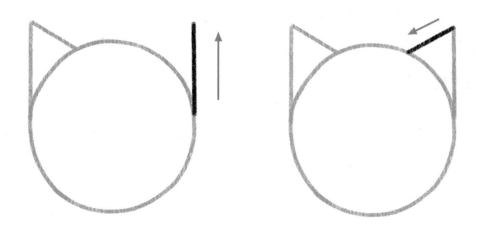

Draw a circle below each ear.

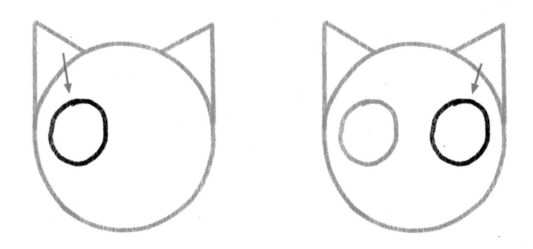

Put a little dot in each circle.

Draw an oval between the circles, and a line down from it.

Add the smile like a segment of lemon and three lines on each cheek.

Draw a box beside the head.

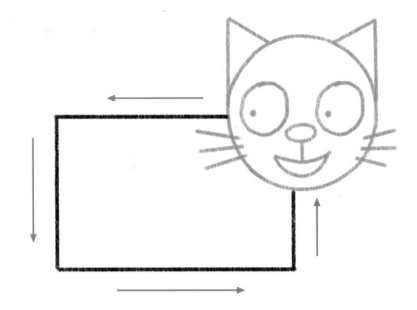

Then add some legs.

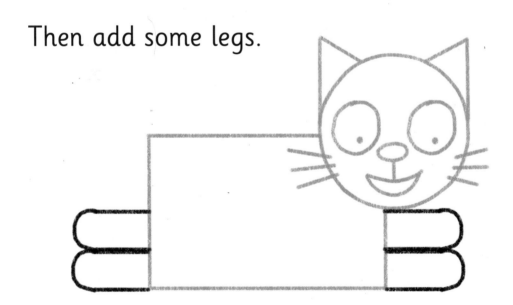

Draw short lines to make the paws.

Don't forget the long, wavy tail!

How to draw Dog

Start with a raindrop shape.

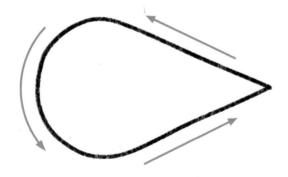

For the left ear, draw a curved line up and
back on the left side.

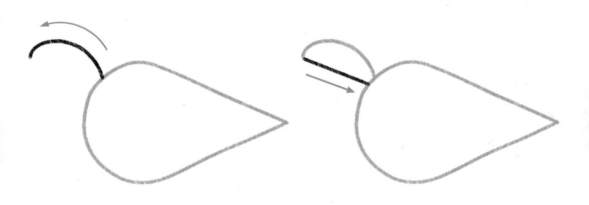

Draw the other ear the same way.

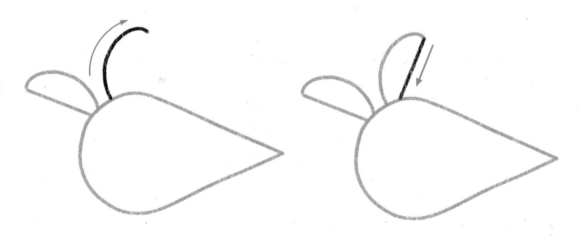

Draw a circle below each ear.

Put little dots inside the circles!

Draw a circle to
make a nose.

Then draw a smile.

Draw a box attached to the head.

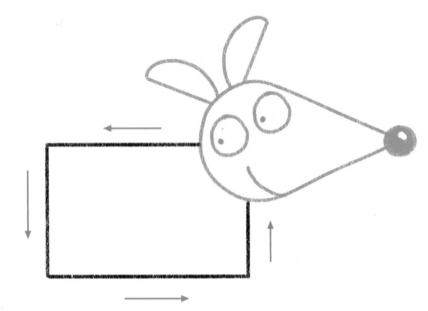

Then add the legs.

Draw short lines to make the paws.

Don't forget the pointy tail!

Dog spies Cat.   Cat spies Dog.

Dog chases Cat down the street.

Zoom! Cat needs to escape from Dog.

But where can Cat hide?

How to draw a tree

Draw a cloud shape.

Fill the cloud shape with leaves.

Draw twiggy bits on your tree.

Finish the twiggy
bits and draw the
trunk all the way
down to the ground.

Draw some little
zigzag lines to make
the roots.

19

Now Cat can disappear high up in the tree!

Dog can see Cat, but he cannot reach her.

Now you can make
your own Cat and Dog
story book!

Drawing Cat and Dog

Cat

Tree

Dog

23

 Review: After reading

Use your assessment from hearing the children read to choose any GPCs, words or tricky words that need additional practice.

Read 1: Decoding

- Ask the children to sound out each of the following words:

  up   some   another

- Ask the children:
  - Can you tell me which sound is the same in each word? (/u/)
  - Can you remember different ways to write the phoneme /u/? Can you point to the grapheme (letter or letters) that make the /u/ sound in each word? (*u, o-e, o*)
  - Can you think of any other words with the /u/ sound in them? (e.g. *under, come, mother*)

Read 2: Prosody

- Model reading each page with expression to the children. After you have read each page, ask the children to have a go at reading with expression.
- Show the children how you read the instructions with appropriate expression.

Read 3: Comprehension

- For every question ask the children how they know the answer. Ask the children:
  - What three things did the book teach you how to draw?
  - Where did Cat hide? (*in the tree*)
  - Would you like to draw any of the things in the book? Which one?
- Why not encourage the children to draw one of the things in the book?